Inside
SPORT

TENNIS

First published in 2008 by Wayland

This paperback edition published in 2012 by Wayland

Copyright © Wayland 2008

Wayland
338 Euston Road
London NW1 3BH

Wayland Australia
Level 17/207 Kent Street
Sydney NSW 2000

Senior Editor: Jennifer Schofield
Designer: Rachel Hamdi and Holly Fulbrook
Illustrator: Ian Thompson and Holly Fulbrook
Picture Researcher: Clive Gifford
Proofreader: Patience Coster

Picture Acknowledgements:
The author and publisher would like to thank the following agencies for allowing these
pictures to be reproduced: cover Clive Brunskill/Getty Images; 1, 41 Odd Andersen/AFP/Getty Images;
3, 24 Ian Walton/Getty Images; 4 Piere Verdy/AFP/Getty Images; Prakash Singh/AFP/Getty Images; 6
Topcial Press Agency/Hulton Archive; 7, 9 Dean Treml/AFP/Getty Images; 8 Jeff Gross/Getty Images; 10,
11 Gerry Penny/AFP/Getty Images; 12 Kristian Dowling/Getty Images; 13 Stuart Franklin/Bengarts/Getty
Images; 15 Jaime Reina/AFP/Getty Images; 16 William West/AFP/Getty Images; 17 John Kelly/Getty
Images; 18 Mark Nolan/Getty Images; 19 Sean Garnsworthy/Getty Images; 20–21 Greg Wood/AFP/Getty
Images; 22 Jimin Lai/AFP/Getty Images; 23, 39 Christophe Simon/AFP/Getty Images; 25 Alexander
Nikolayev/AFP/Getty Images; 26, 33 William West/AFP/Getty Images; 27 Julian Finney/Getty Images; 28
Ryan Pierse/Getty Images; 29 Carl de Souza/AFP/Getty Images; 30 Al Bello/Getty Images; 31 Phil
Walter/Getty Images; 32 Gary M Prior/Getty Images; 34 Jack Guez/AFP/Getty Images; Matthew
Stockman/Getty Images; 35 Mark Ralston/AFP/Getty Images; 37 Nick Laham/Getty Images; 42 Jamie
Squire/Getty Images; 43 Timothy A Clary/AFP/Getty Images; 44 AFP/Getty Images; 45 top Jean-Loup
Gautreau/AFP/Getty Images; 45 bottom Mike Hewitt//Getty Images; 46 Wish List

CIP data
Gifford, Clive
  Tennis. - (Inside sport)
  1. Tennis - Juvenile fiction
  I. Title
  796.3'42

ISBN: 978 0 7502 6950 6

Printed in China   796·342

Wayland is a division of Hachette Children's Books, an Hachette UK company
www.hachette.co.uk

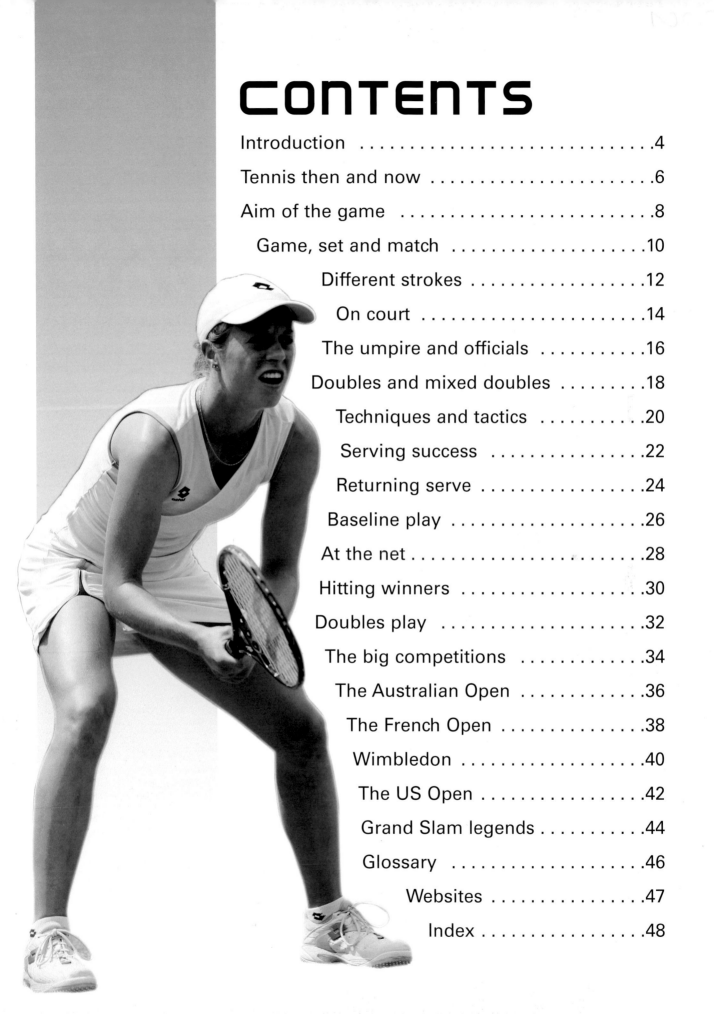

CONTENTS

INTRODUCTION

Tennis is an explosive, all-action sport that makes great demands on a player's fitness, skill, decision-making abilities and power. It is a sport played by millions of people of all ages and abilities around the world.

The Game

Tennis is a game that pits either individuals against each other in singles matches, or two against two in doubles and mixed doubles matches. Players use their rackets to stroke and power a ball around a rectangular court, trying to score a winning shot or force their opponent into making a mistake. Top players have a large range of shots they can play, from thumping forehand drives to delicate drop shots that just creep over the net. Players also need outstanding athleticism to move rapidly around the court. Their lightning-quick reactions enable them to deal with balls that can fly towards them at speeds of well over 100km/h.

MAD FACT

In 1977, Denise Panagopoulou of Greece represented her country in the Federation Cup (see p35) against Portugal. She was just 12 years old!

Argentinean David Nalbandian stretches for a ball at the French Open.

Young and Old

With some 35,000 tennis courts in Britain alone, anyone armed with a racket and ball can play tennis. Many children start to play junior versions of the game with foam balls. These games, such as Mini Tennis in Australia and Ariel Mini Tennis in Britain, are played on smaller courts or half a regular tennis court. For young players who really get into the game, there is a large network of junior competitions in which they can take part.

Top players tend to peak early, especially in the women's game where many of its star players, such as Serena Williams or Maria Sharapova, have won major tournaments by the age of 16 or 17. In 2007, Kim Clijsters, the former world number one and winner of 34 major tournament titles including the 2005 US Open, retired at the tender age of 23. At the other end of the spectrum, many players continue playing for fun or in veterans or champions tournaments well into their fifties and sixties.

Leander Paes and Mahesh Bhupathi shake hands with Jonas Bjorkman and Simon Aspelin after their doubles match ends.

Fun and Friendly

Whether the match is in a local park or is the final of a major tournament, players are expected to behave cordially towards each other and towards the officials who run the match and any spectators present. Tennis etiquette is an important part of the culture of the game. Top players may occasionally lose their tempers in the middle of an epic match, but they will always congratulate their opponents at the net as the match ends. Players are also expected to play some warm-up shots (known as a knock up) with their opponents before a match.

TENNIS THEN AND NOW

Tennis began in the nineteenth century as a pastime for the wealthy, fully dressed in the regular fashions of the time. It was seen as a game for amateurs until the arrival of the Open Era in 1968, which allowed professional (paid to play) players to enter all tournaments.

MAD FACT

Tennis appeared at the very first modern Olympics in 1896. An Irish tourist visiting Greece, John Pius Boland, picked up a racket and won the competition!

Tennis Clothing

In the past, men played in long trousers and, sometimes, jackets. Women wore dresses that covered their arms and legs. Today, male tennis players wear lightweight shirts and shorts while women wear dresses or skirts and tops that are designed to be breathable. Players may change their clothing several times during a long match. Footwear is important, and players wear tennis shoes that support their feet when they move sideways and absorb some of the shock of the impact on the ground.

Rackets and Balls

Early tennis rackets were made from wood and the head, the part of the racket where the strings are, was quite small. Aluminium rackets, which were lighter than wood, were introduced in the 1970s. Today, rackets are made from advanced materials, including carbon fibre and graphite. Modern rackets have a bigger head than those used in the past and can help to generate huge amounts of power.

Tennis balls are made of a hollow rubber core covered in a nylon or woollen shell. Tournament balls are filled with pressurized air to aid their bounce. In tournaments, the balls are changed regularly as with use, they lose a little of their speed and bounce. At a major tournament, such as Wimbledon, the balls are changed after the first seven games and then after every nine games.

French tennis legend, Suzanne Lenglen shocked society in the 1920s by wearing shorter dresses and showing off her bare arms to give her more freedom of movement.

The Open Era

The first professional tour was organized in 1926 by C.C. Pyle. Famous players of the time, such as Suzanne Lenglen, were paid to play exhibition matches. As soon as a player turned professional, he or she was barred from taking part in amateur tournaments, including all four Grand Slam events (Wimbledon and the Australian, US and French Opens). In 1968, amateur tournaments began to accept professionals and what is known as the Open Era began.

Today, thousands of professional or semi-professional tennis players compete in different levels of tournament. The Women's Tennis Association (WTA) organizes women's professional tennis, while the men's game is run by the Association of Tennis Professionals (ATP). The International Tennis Federation (ITF) runs the Grand Slams, team competitions and tours for juniors and players below the main professional tour standard. With prize money measured in hundreds of thousands for the top tournaments and with lucrative sponsorship deals, the top male and female players are millionaires many times over.

Fitter and Faster

The professional era has seen players become fitter, tougher and more powerful. Top players need to have the stamina – the ability to work hard over long periods – to play for a whole season, which runs from January to the start of November. The closed season sees players working on their core fitness in the gym, training outdoors and practising under the watchful eyes of their coach, personal trainer and physiotherapist. As well as stamina, top players also need explosive speed off the mark, strength to hit powerful shots and the flexibility to stretch and reach the ball.

Chilean Fernando Gonzalez grimaces with pain during an injury time-out. Injuries can be treated, but sometimes players have to retire and forfeit the match.

AIM OF THE GAME

Tennis is a sport where players aim to win points. Each point begins with one player playing the ball over the net, which runs across the middle of the tennis court, and into the other player's half of the court. This is called a serve. The player receiving the serve must try to return the ball over the net and into his opponent's half of the court. The ball is then hit to and fro by the players until the point is won or lost.

Serving

The server serves for an entire game. He or she starts by serving the ball from behind the baseline at the back of the court. For the first point, the server also stands to the right of a small line on the baseline called the centre mark. The player throws the ball up and then hits it with an overhead swing of the racket so that it passes over the net without touching it. The ball must first bounce in the opponent's half of the court inside the large box diagonally opposite, called the service court.

If the ball touches the net and lands in the service court, the umpire calls a first service and the player has to serve again. However, if the ball hits the net and falls on the server's side of the court or if it does not land inside the correct service court, then a fault is called.

MAD //// //// FACT

Venus Williams served 33 double faults in the Ladies Singles in Wimbledon in 2007 more than any other woman player, yet she still won the tournament.

centre mark

baseline

Rafael Nadal is about to serve with his feet behind the baseline and to the left of the centre mark. His serve must travel over the net and land in the right-hand service court.

The server has up to two chances to serve the point. If the second serve is a fault too, then a double fault occurs and the server loses the point. Serves are taken alternately from the right and left of the centre mark until the game is over. When the game is over, the other player then has a chance to serve.

Tommy Robredo falls over the net after returning a shot against David Ferrer at the 2007 Heineken Open in New Zealand.

MAD FACT

In the 2005 Pacific Life Open, Roger Federer and Lleyton Hewitt took part in one of the greatest ever rallies. It lasted 45 shots and featured lobs, drop shots and diving volleys.

Rallying

Once the ball has been served and returned, a rally is underway. Players must hit the ball before it bounces twice on their side of the court. A player does not have to let the ball bounce at all and can choose instead to hit it in mid-air, known as a volley. Some rallies are just three or four shots, but others can be an energy-sapping 20-shots. The rally ends when one of the players hits the ball into the net, fails to reach the ball and it bounces twice, or hits the ball out of the court. A rally can also be lost if a player hits the ball twice in a row or touches the net.

GAME, SET AND MATCH

Tennis has a unique scoring system, with points, games, sets and matches. It can sound confusing to the beginner, but it is, in fact, fairly straightforward to learn.

Points and Games

It can take as few as four points to win a game. Points are scored 15, 30, 40 and game. The server's score is given first, so if the score is 30–15, then the server has two points and his or her opponent has just one. If a player has not scored a point in a game, his score is given as 'love'. If both players win three points in a game, the score is 40–40, or 'deuce'. To win the game from this score, a player has to win two points in a row. The first point is known as advantage. If the player with advantage wins the next point, he or she wins the game. If he or she loses the point, the score goes back to deuce. Players change ends after the first game of a set and then after every two games. Professional players are allowed a 90-second break between end changes.

Goran Ivanesevic powers down a serve in the fifth set of his 2001 Wimbledon semi-final against Tim Henman. The scoreboard shows that the second and fourth sets both went to tiebreakers (7–6).

Sets and Tiebreakers

Sets last until one player reaches at least six games and is two games ahead of his or her opponent. Women's matches are usually the best of three sets (the first player to have two sets) while men's matches are either best of three or best of five sets (the first player to have three sets). In the past, players continued each set until one player was two games ahead. This led to some very long matches – for example, John McEnroe and Mats Wilander's 1982 Davis Cup match included a 32-game third set and lasted six-and-a-half hours.

The tiebreaker system was introduced to reduce the length of matches. Players tied at six games all play a game of first to seven points. If that is tied at six points all, the winner of the tiebreak is the first player to win two points in a row. The US Open (see page 42) uses this system for all sets but other tournaments use it for all apart from the last set, where the two-games-clear rule applies.

(see page 42)

Who is...

...Martina Navratilova?

Martina Navratilova is the most successful woman tennis player ever. A pioneer of dedication and fitness, she won a staggering 59 Grand Slam titles (18 singles, 31 doubles and 10 mixed doubles). In singles, she was untouchable for many years, winning 1,442 matches and scooping 167 singles titles as well as 177 women's doubles titles. She won her tenth mixed doubles title in 2006 when she was almost 50 years old.

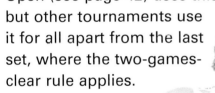

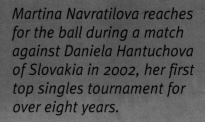

Martina Navratilova reaches for the ball during a match against Daniela Hantuchova of Slovakia in 2002, her first top singles tournament for over eight years.

DIFFERENT STROKES

Tennis players need speed and agility to get close enough to the ball to hit it, and a range of different shots to allow for the ball to reach their opponents at different heights and angles. Top players have a large array of shots, from drop shots that just creep over the net, to thundering forehand drives that zoom down the line.

Martina Hingis plays a two-handed backhand volley, aiming to punch the ball over the net and away from her opponent.

Groundstrokes and Volleys

Shots played after the ball has bounced are known as groundstrokes. Shots played in mid-air before the ball has bounced are called volleys. Volleys are mostly played close to the net. One exception is the overhead smash, which can be hit from many positions on the court. The smash is used when the ball has risen high and the receiving player is in position to hit it really hard with the racket over his or her head.

Forehand and Backhand

Forehand shots are played on the racket-arm side of a player. The forehand drive is a groundstroke that can become a player's most powerful shot as he or she stands side-on to the ball and swings freely through it. Backhand shots are played on the opposite side, with the player's racket arm crossing his or her body as it swings. Backhand drives are played with one or two hands on the racket handle. They are harder than forehands to perfect, but just as crucial.

?

Who is...

...Roger Federer?

The finest stroke-maker of the current generation of players, Roger Federer from Switzerland has been ranked world number one since February 2004. An incredibly versatile player, able to play at the net or baseline, Federer's supreme range of strokes is beautiful to watch but deadly to play against. He won his first Grand Slam, Wimbledon, in 2003 and since then has added an astonishing 16 more grand slams.

Balance, Position and Timing

Players use different grips for different shots and can change their precise grip extremely quickly during a rally. To execute a good shot, players need awareness to anticipate where the ball will head, good footwork to move into the perfect position to play the shot, and the ability to control and time the swing of the racket head. Some shots, such as a forehand groundstroke from the back of the court, require a full swing of the racket with a long follow-through to generate power. Other shots, such as volleys, may have a very short swing and follow-through as the ball is stunned or punched back across the net. Whatever the type of shot, a player needs excellent balance and the ability to time the shot well.

Roger Federer keeps his eye on the ball as he whips his racket head through to play a forehand groundstroke.

ON COURT

Tennis is played on the same sized court throughout the world. A court measures 23.77m long by 8.23m wide for singles matches. For doubles, the outer sidelines are used to make the court 10.97m wide. The rear of each end of the court is marked out by the baseline. The other court markings mark out the service courts (also called service boxes) into which players must serve accurately.

Net Gains

The net is strung across the middle of the court on posts. Next to the posts, the net stands 1.07m high but in the middle of the court it should be 0.91m high. There is no penalty if during a rally, a player hits the ball and it clips the net but falls on to his or her opponent's side of the court. Players tend to wave a hand to their opponent to acknowledge their luck when this happens.

In or Out?

The white lines that mark out a tennis court are considered to be part of the court. If any part of the ball bounces on any part of the line, then the ball is said to be in play. During high-speed rallies, the ball can zoom around the court at over 100km/h, so it can be hard for spectators or players to spot whether the ball has touched the line or if it is genuinely out. With matches turning on a single point, making the right decisions is crucial and top tournaments employ both human officials and electronic equipment (see page 17).

1. Baseline
2. Sideline (singles)
3. Sideline (doubles)
4. Service line
5. Centre service line
6. Left-hand service box
7. Right-hand service box

On a typical tennis court, the baseline can be up to 10cm thick and the centre service line 5cm wide. All other lines are between 2.5 and 5cm wide.

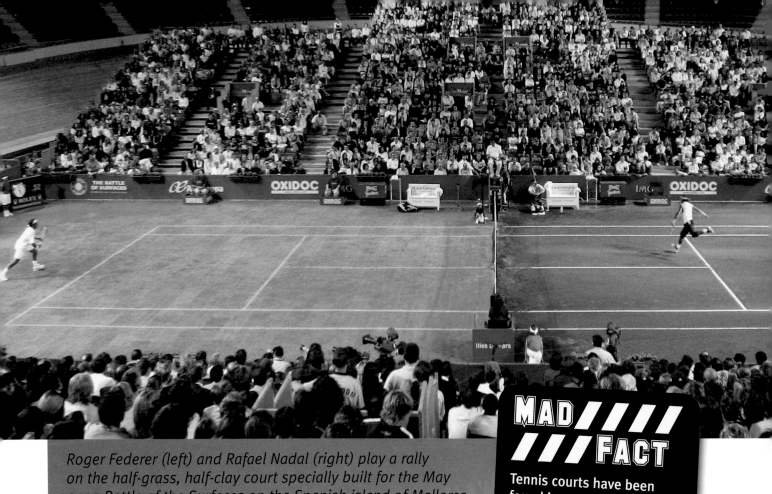

Roger Federer (left) and Rafael Nadal (right) play a rally on the half-grass, half-clay court specially built for the May 2007 Battle of the Surfaces on the Spanish island of Mallorca. Nadal eventually won the three-set match, 7–5 4–6 7–6.

MAD FACT

Tennis courts have been found in strange places – for example on the converted helipad of Dubai's Burj Al Arab's Hotel, which is 200m tall and juts out over the ocean. Roger Federer and Andre Agassi played a friendly game on this court prior to the 2005 Dubai Open.

Different Surfaces

The material used to make tennis courts varies greatly. When tennis first started it was played only on grass, but this has changed. Today, only Wimbledon and some professional tournaments held just before Wimbledon are still played on grass. Each surface has different characteristics, affecting the speed and bounce of the ball, and this impacts greatly on players' tactics and styles of play.

Clay is the slowest of the surfaces used. It encourages longer rallies and shrewd tactical play, as players try to pull each other around the court searching for an opening. Clay also requires players to be exceptionally fit to cover so much ground in many long rallies. Some players are highly skilled at skidding or sliding with their feet across the loose clay surface. Grass can be fast and, with its unpredictable bounce, favours powerful, hard-hitting players. Hard courts, such as those used at the US Open, have a true bounce which can mean that players' shots can often be predicted by their opponents unless they have great variety and can disguise what type of shot they are playing.

THE UMPIRE AND OFFICIALS

Most tennis matches are casual affairs where the two players judge decisions such as whether the ball was in or not. In competitive tennis, matches are controlled by an umpire, with the assistance of a range of other officials.

Marat Safin argues fiercely with the umpire during his 2007 Australian Open match against Andy Roddick.

People on Court

The edges of a court at a major championship can appear to be crowded. Apart from the umpire, there is a collection of officials, each with a specific job. A net judge is perched alongside the net and has the job of signalling whether a serve clips the net on the way through. Line judges are positioned around the edges of the court. Each one monitors a single line to determine whether the ball lands in or out. In addition to these officials, there is a collection of ball girls and boys. They field balls that have landed in the net or have gone wide, and roll them to other ball boys or girls in the corners of the court area so that they can supply balls to the server.

The Umpire and Referee

The umpire usually sits in a high chair on the edge of the court. From here, he or she has an excellent view of the court below. The umpire's duties include making sure that new balls are delivered and ends are changed at the right time. The umpire also times breaks so that delays in play do not occur. He or she calls the score after each

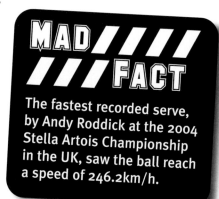

MAD //// //// FACT

The fastest recorded serve, by Andy Roddick at the 2004 Stella Artois Championship in the UK, saw the ball reach a speed of 246.2km/h.

Who is...

...John McEnroe?

Famous for his fiery temper, which brought him into many confrontations with umpires, John McEnroe was also a supreme competitor and a magnificent player. Boasting a wonderful touch, he could conjure great shots out of nowhere and was a brilliant volleyer at the net. He had famous rivalries with Bjorn Borg and Jimmy Connors on his way to seven Grand Slam singles titles and nine doubles titles, partnered mostly by Peter Fleming. McEnroe also won the 1977 French Open mixed doubles with Mary Carillo. An illustrious career, which brought him 76 singles titles and 70 doubles titles, included an astonishing 2006 ATP tour win with Jonas Bjorkman at age 47.

point is played and announces who wins each game. On occasion, umpires may overrule one of the line judge's decisions or order a point to be played again. This is called a let and it happens when a serve is hit before the receiver is ready or if some unusual interruption occurs, such as an intruder on court. Occasionally, players lose their tempers and umpires may have to award a penalty point as a punishment.

Electronic Aids

In recent years, electronic systems equipped with high-speed sensors have been introduced to aid the umpire and officials. Cyclops was the first system, appearing in 1981. A high-pitched beep sounds if the ball lands outside the service box. In 2006, an instant-replay system, called Hawk-Eye, was adopted at the US Open. In 2007, at the Australian Open and at Wimbledon players were allowed a set number of challenges for points they disputed.

John McEnroe focuses on the ball as he serves with his wooden racket in the early 1980s.

DOUBLES AND MIXED DOUBLES

Italy's Tatiana Garbin crouches close to the net as her partner, Tina Krizan of Slovakia, serves during the Canberra Women's Tennis Classic in 2005.

Doubles is an exciting team game for pairs of men, women, or in mixed doubles, one man and one woman. The basic rules and scoring system are the same as in singles matches, but in a doubles match the court is wider and there are differences in serving rules and positional play.

Doubles Serving

Serving in doubles is more complicated than it is in singles as it has to be in a specific order, with each player serving one in four games. One team's players serve every first and third game, and the other team's players serve every second and fourth game. If the ball touches the server's partner's body, clothing or racket, then the serve is a fault. If the serve is good, but it touches the receiver's partner in any way, then the serving pair wins the point. In tiebreakers, the player whose turn it is to serve next serves the first point, then the service order continues, with each player serving two points until the tiebreaker is decided.

As soon as the ball is served and then returned by the receiver, any player can hit the ball, just as long as only one player from a pair hits the ball before it crosses the net. During a long doubles rally, players may have to exchange positions to make sure they cover as much of the court as possible. It can all add up to fast, frenetic entertainment for spectators and a great challenge to a player's judgement and shot-making skills.

Who are...

...The Williams Sisters?

Separated by just a year in age, the US Williams sisters, Serena and Venus, have had an enormous impact on women's tennis. Venus has seven Grand Slam singles titles and Serena has eight. Playing together, the hard-serving, powerfully athletic sisters prove formidable opponents, and have won seven Grand Slam doubles and an Olympic gold medal in 2000. Venus did the double by winning the Olympic singles the same year. Serena won five of her singles Grand Slams in 2002 and 2003, all of which saw her beat her elder sister in the final.

Serena Williams (right) looks on as her sister, Venus, looks to play a backhand volley at the 2003 Australian Open.

Positions, Please

Doubles pairs have to decide on their positioning in different ways. At the most basic level, it means choosing which side of the court (left or right) a player will mostly play from. A right-handed player with a strong backhand tends to play on the left, as does a left-handed player with a strong forehand. During serving, the server's partner can stand in a range of positions. He or she can be aggressive, and stand crouched near the net, or stand further back if his or her partner has a weak serve or is playing a second serve.

STAT ATTACK

ITF Men's Doubles World Champions

2010 Bob Bryan (USA) / Mike Bryan (USA)

2009 Bob Bryan (USA) / Mike Bryan (USA)

2008 Daniel Nestor (Canada) / Nenad Zimonjic (Serbia)

2007 Bob Bryan (USA) / Mike Bryan (USA)

2006 Bob Bryan (USA) / Mike Bryan (USA)

2005 Bob Bryan (USA) / Mike Bryan (USA)

2004 Bob Bryan (USA) / Mike Bryan (USA)

2003 Bob Bryan (USA) / Mike Bryan (USA)

2002 Daniel Nestor (Canada) / Mark Knowles (Bahamas)

2001 Jonas Bjorkman (Sweden) / Todd Woodbridge (Australia)

2000 Todd Woodbridge (Australia) / Mark Woodforde (Australia)

TECHNIQUES AND TACTICS

To succeed, tennis players need to possess a great range of shots, supreme fitness and a clear idea of the way they intend to play – their tactics or game plan. Tactics may have to change from match to match depending on the opponent or the court surface and conditions. Tactics may also change during a game, depending on how a player and opponent are performing.

Player and Coach

Players work with their coaches to develop their tactics. Many top players are close to their coaches who travel to tournaments with them and supervise training and practice away from tournaments. In team competitions, such as the Davis Cup (see page 35), the team's other players and their coaches often sit alongside the court and can give encouragement and advice to players between games. In most other tournaments though, on-court coaching during a match is forbidden.

MAD /// /// /// FACT

In 1998, an unknown Lleyton Hewitt was ranked the world number 550 when he won the Adelaide International tournament. He is the lowest ranked winner of a major men's competition.

Exploiting Weaknesses

Players and coaches do their homework on upcoming opponents, analyzing their strengths and weaknesses. Some of these can be obvious, for example a player may be renowned for his or her formidable serve or for not being quick around the court. Others can be more subtle, for example an opponent may note that in the later sets of a match a player tends to favour his or her forehand side or stops hitting certain types of shots. Players try to find ways to target their own strengths and their opponent's weaknesses.

Maria Sharapova hits a two-handed backhand overhead shot, one of the hardest strokes in tennis.

Mental Attitude

Players need confidence and high levels of concentration throughout a match to focus and analyze their opponents' game and their own, and to make adjustments to how they are playing. Positive thinking can help a player recover from being one set or two sets down, but to succeed a player must be totally committed. Top players never give up in a game or, indeed, a rally. They need to chase down every shot and try to keep the ball in play. Many points are won because a player has managed to retrieve the ball from an almost impossible position, and gradually got back into the point.

Conditioning And Preparation

Tennis is a tough sport and no amount of tactics can compensate for a player who is not at peak fitness. Players train hard away from tournaments and prepare carefully before each match, so that their bodies can perform throughout a long, gruelling series of sets. Many players retire from matches when they feel a muscle pull or some other problem, to avoid making an injury worse. Players expect to lose litres of liquid from their bodies during a match and regularly top up with small amounts of water or special energy drinks.

STAT ATTACK

Recent ITF World Champions

The International Tennis Federation (ITF) picks world champions each year.

Year	Men's Singles	Women's Singles
2010	Rafael Nadal	Jelena Jankovic
2009	Roger Federer	Serena Williams
2008	Rafael Nadal	Caroline Wozniacki
2007	Roger Federer	Justine Henin
2006	Roger Federer	Justine Henin
2005	Roger Federer	Kim Clijsters
2004	Roger Federer	Anastasia Myskina
2003	Andy Roddick	Justine Henin
2002	Lleyton Hewitt	Serena Williams
2001	Lleyton Hewitt	Jennifer Capriati

SERVING SUCCESS

Serving sees the player toss the ball up high and then bring the racket up and over to connect with the ball, sending it speeding away. Serving is not just a way to get the ball into play. In the modern game, it is one of a player's main weapons.

Serving Tactics

Professional players work constantly on their service action so that it is as smooth and easy to repeat as possible. The aim of the service action is to transfer as much of the player's body movement as is possible into power in the racket head. Accuracy is important, too. Top players do not aim just to get the ball in the service box, they want to place their serve deep (as close to the service line as possible) to give their opponents less time to react and to generate difficult bounce. Common targets are the two corners of the service box furthest from the net.

Servers can also adjust how their racket head connects with the ball to generate different types of spin. The slice serve sees the racket come across the back of the ball to generate sideways spin. This means that when the ball bounces, it tends to slide away from the receiver. The topspin serve sees the ball dip just before landing, and then it kicks up again.

Alicia Molik of Australia follows through as she powers away a serve.

Players try to be aggressive on their first serve but, if it is a fault, they need a guaranteed second serve, usually with less pace and placed less aggressively, to stay in the point.

Ace!

When a player serves the ball and wins the point without the opponent touching it, this is called an ace. It is sometimes thought that only male players hit aces, but today's top female stars can also generate them. Amélie Mauresmo, for example, hit 35 aces during Wimbledon 2006 on her way to winning the women's singles title. Like all good serves, hitting an ace requires power but also accuracy and spin to place the ball as far away from the opponent as possible.

Foot Faults and Double Faults

A foot fault is another way in which a player can serve a fault. It happens when, as the player strikes the ball, he or she touches the baseline with his or her foot or is standing on the wrong side of the baseline centre mark. A foot fault counts the same as any regular fault.

After two faults, a player is said to have double faulted and loses the point. Players making a lot of double faults can put themselves under huge pressure as they are giving away 'free' points to their opponent. In contrast, Roger Federer did the opposite of this, by hitting only five double faults and serving 68 aces on his seven-match march to win the 2006 Wimbledon men's singles title.

Andy Roddick arches his back as he hits a big serve. Top players, such as Roddick, work hard on disguising their serve, making it difficult for their opponent to work out where they are going to hit the ball and with what spin.

RETURNING SERVE

At the top level, the player serving has a major advantage. He or she controls the start of each point and a fast serve can take just half a second to reach the receiving player. The receiver (sometimes known as the returner) has to react quickly and choose the right option. Players such as Andre Agassi, Lleyton Hewitt and Andy Murray are renowned as returners of serve. They are able to react quickly and put the server under pressure.

The Ready Position

Receivers tend to stand a little behind the baseline, in position so that they can cover serves hit on either side of them. They take up a ready position awaiting the serve, facing the net square-on with the racket out in front of them. They stay on their toes, ready to move or spring in any direction. Their eyes are focused on the server as they check the ball toss, racket angle and any other signs of where the serve might be heading. Receivers tend to position themselves more aggressively when their opponent is playing a second serve. They may stand closer to, on or even inside the baseline.

STAT ATTACK

Break Points Won at Wimbledon 2006

Men		Women	
Roger Federer	35	Justine Henin	35
Jonas Bjorkman	28	Amélie Mauresmo	30
Lleyton Hewitt	27	Elena Dementieva	30
Marcos Baghdatis	27	Maria Sharapova	25
Radek Stepanek	25	Kim Clijsters	24

Germany's Martina Muller is in a well-balanced ready position with her head up and eyes focused on her opponent as she serves.

Blocking or Attacking

The minimum aim for returning serve is to reach the ball and send it back so that it is in play and a rally can begin. When a serve puts the returner under a lot of pressure, the player may stretch out his or her racket and simply try to block the ball so that it bounces back into the opponent's half of the court. Top players often aim for more than just blocking the ball. They are aiming to get on top in the point from the start. A short or weak serve might see the ball sit up nicely for the receiver to move forward and play an attacking shot. Depending on where the serve lands, this could be a powerful cross-court shot (a shot travelling diagonally across the court) or, if their opponent is moving towards the net, a ball hit back at their feet sometimes forcing an error.

MAD//// ////FACT

In 2006, Brenda Schultz-McCarthy hit the fastest ever recorded serve by a woman. Her 209km/h serve beat Venus Williams' 1998 record of 205km/h.

Swede Thomas Johansson stretches to get his racket on the ball to return a serve hit by Mario Ancic.

Breaking Serve

Servers expect to hold their serve (win the game in which they are serving). Therefore it is a great advantage for the receiver if he or she manages to break serve and win that game. Even at 30–0 or 40–0 down, receivers try their hardest to get back into the game. Many breaks of serve have occurred after the receiver has won the first points in the game, only to be followed by the receiver winning the next series of points. Break point is the crucial moment: if the receiver wins the point, he or she wins the game. Playing break points well is a matter of nerve for both server and receiver and players must choose the right shot to play and execute it well. A game that results in a break of serve is followed by a high-pressure game in which the broken player strains every sinew to break back immediately.

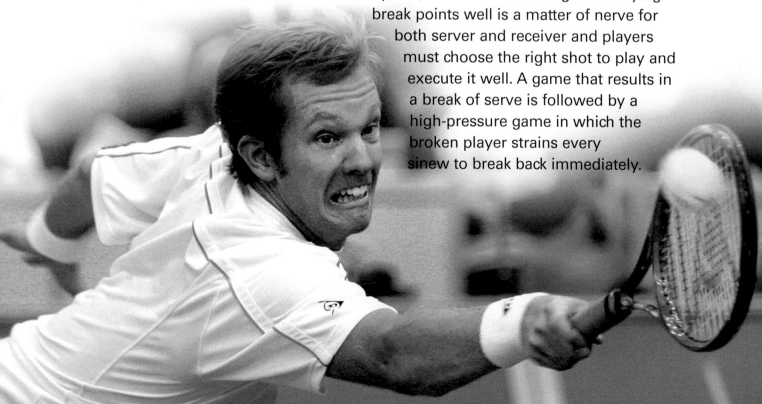

BASELINE PLAY

In many points in a match, both players may stay around the baseline, playing their shots from the back of the court. Baseline play occurs on all court surfaces, but is especially popular on clay and other slower surfaces that make it hard to serve and volley. A baseline rally may end in a winner, an error or one player moving in towards the net.

Rallies

Baseline rallies are a tussle for position and opportunity between players. From the baseline, players can hit strong groundstrokes, aiming to move their opponent out of position and trying to play to their own strengths and their opponent's weaknesses. Patience is important as players wait for an opening to attempt a shot that wins the point. Players are mindful of playing 'percentage tennis', taking risks only when necessary. For example, hitting shots down the line is riskier than playing cross-court strokes because the net is 15cm higher at the net posts than it is in the centre.

Belgian former world number one, Kim Clijsters reaches for a backhand shot from just behind the baseline.

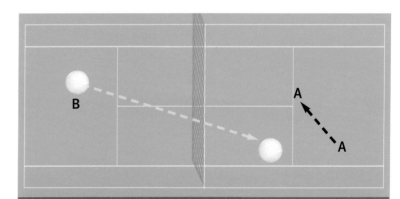

With Player A out wide, Player B uses a popular attacking tactic. Instead of hitting into the space on the court, Player B hits the ball to where Player A was originally. Player A has begun sprinting back to cover the space and is wrongfooted by Player B's return.

One Shot Ahead

When rallying from the baseline, professional players often think one or more shots ahead. They aim to think of shots in terms of combinations. One such combination starts with the player hitting the ball cross-court with slice spin (see page 22) on the ball. This sends the ball and opponent out wide to one side of the court. When this is returned, the second shot can be a straight drive down the opposite side, well out of the opponent's reach.

Pouncing on Errors

During a long baseline rally, one player is likely to hit a poorer shot or find him or herself a long way from the ideal position on the court. These are often the best moments for opponents to attack. A short shot, for example, can allow the returner to move forward and either play a winner or hit a deep angled shot that gives him or her time to get to the net to make a volley.

Who is...

...Rafael Nadal?

A hugely exciting player, Spanish star Rafael Nadal uses his enormous power to great effect at the baseline, and is able to hit searing groundstrokes. The winner of 21 ATP titles before he turned 21, Nadal is also lightning fast around the court.

At Wimbledon 2006, Nadal surprised some critics by changing his game at that tournament and coming into the net more. Although he has had to come second to Roger Federer at many Grand Slam tournaments, Nadal is considered the king of clay-court tennis and is unbeaten at the French Open, where he has won four titles in a row. In 2008, he battled Federer to win Wimbledon in a thrilling final.

Rafael Nadal plays an overhead smash. Nadal is a baseliner but can mix up his game; this was demonstrated by how hard he pushed Federer in the 2007 Wimbledon final.

AT THE NET

Players may choose to come in towards the net to attack or, sometimes, a very short shot from their opponent may force them to come in. In either case, the net player takes a risk of losing the point via a lob or a passing shot. But they may also gain the chance to win the point quickly with a volley.

Volleying

Volleys are shots hit either on the backhand or forehand side before the ball has bounced. Volleys are hit with a shorter and faster swing than groundstrokes, and are punched through with a firm wrist. Many volleys take place with the ball at waist height or higher. These need to be directed down over the net and into the opponent's court. Low volleys, when the racket meets the ball below net height, can be hard shots to master. Skilled volleyers may sometimes look as if they mean to hit a hard volley deep into the court, but instead tilt the racket head at the last minute and play a more delicate volley cross-court.

Tim Henman moves to the side and towards the net to make a backhand volley.

Amélie Mauresmo watches the ball onto the racket as she makes a backhand volley.

Who is...

...Amélie Mauresmo?

France's Amélie Mauresmo is a former world number 1. She is a powerful server who frequently comes into the net after her serve to make winning volleys. Mauresmo burst on to the scene in 1999 when she was unseeded, yet reached the final of the Australian Open. She reached the semi-finals of Wimbledon three times before finally winning the competition in 2006. She also won the Australian Open in 2006 and has 24 WTA singles tour titles, as well as a silver medal at the 2004 Olympics.

Risks And Rewards

Coming to the net can disrupt an opponent's natural game, and may see him or her make an unforced error as he or she strains to hit the ball too hard or too wide of the player at the net. A volley at the net gives an opponent very little time to react and, directed deep or angled away from the opponent, it can be impossible to reach. However, coming to the net carries risks. If the player does not get to the net in time or if his or her shot before moving to the net is weak, then he or she runs the risk of the opponent hitting a passing shot out of reach.

The Lob

Lobs sail high in the air, over the head of the player at or moving in towards the net. The ball should be out of reach but instead drops down in court close to the baseline. Lobs can be used defensively or in attack. In defence, a player struggling to reach the ball or having been pulled out wide may use a high, defensive lob to force the other player back to the baseline and buy time to get back into a good position. In attack, a lob can be hit with a lot of topspin. This sends the ball over the net player, after which it dips sharply and may bounce twice before the net player can reach it.

MAD FACT

In the first round of the 2004 French Open, Fabrice Santoro won his match against Arnaud Clement. The match was played mainly from the baseline and took 6 hours and 33 minutes to complete.

HITTING WINNERS

Some rallies end when players make errors such as hitting the ball into the net or out of the court. Other rallies end as a result of one player hitting a superb winner which his or her opponent has no way of returning.

Perfect Position

Moving an opponent around a court helps to generate the space and angles to play potentially winning shots. At the same time, players try to stay aware of where they are and use quick footwork to move into the best position for their next shot. Players work hard to avoid finding themselves in no-man's land, the area around the service line also known as the mid- or half-court area. In this position, they are rarely close enough to the net to make a winning volley and they leave large areas of space behind, into which their opponents can hit.

Surprise and Disguise

Throughout a match, players try to read their opponents' game so that they can anticipate what they will do next. Players rarely attempt a truly outrageous surprise shot, but they do try to disguise what shot they intend to play in order to outwit their opponents. A classic example of this is when a player looks as though he or she is about to hit a groundstroke down the line but at the last moment whips his or her wrist around to angle the shot cross-court. The opponent trying to anticipate the shot may already be moving or leaning in one direction when the ball starts to head in another direction.

Mary Pierce angles her racket back to play a backhand drop shot.

Drop Shots

Many tactics and strokes require disguise, and the drop shot is a classic example. A drop shot is very softly hit, with the racket travelling underneath the ball. It is often hit with disguise, when an opponent is a long way from the net or is very tired. The effect of a good drop shot is to slow down the ball dramatically so that it travels just over the net. When it bounces, backspin put on the ball by the shot can make it stop dead rather than bounce forwards. Even if the opponent lunges and reaches the ball, there is a good chance he or she will be unbalanced and leave much of the court free for a winner to be played.

Smashing!

If a high, short ball sails upwards, a good player gets into position quickly to play a smash. The most spectacular shot in tennis, the overhead smash sees players throw their bodyweight into the shot so that they strike a high ball overhead with the full force of the racket. As with serving, power is vital but control, the angle of the racket and the placement of the ball are even more so. A controlled smash directed away from the other player will often win the point.

Roger Federer leaps high to generate a lot of power as he throws his racket into making a powerful overhead smash.

DOUBLES PLAY

Whether their game involves putting away a high ball with a powerful smash or serving well, doubles players often use similar tactics and techniques to singles players. However, with two players a side and a bigger court, there are other tactics that good doubles pairs have to take into account, too.

Partner and Opponents

A doubles pair needs to communicate clearly and frequently to get the most out of the game. This includes encouraging a partner when he or she is struggling. Players need to be aware of each other's strengths and weaknesses as well as those of their opponents. In professional doubles, a player is rarely weaker than his or her partner in all parts of the game. A player may be a weak server but have a superb volley. He or she may also be weaker on their forehand side than their backhand. In competitive doubles, pairs aim to learn and target opponents' weaknesses as often as possible.

?

Who are...

...Todd Woodbridge and Mark Woodforde?

Australian tennis players Mark Woodforde and Todd Woodbridge formed a successful partnership on court that took them to 11 Grand Slam doubles titles, including five Wimbledons in a row (1993–97) and Olympic gold in 1996. Woodforde retired in 2000 but Woodbridge enjoyed further success, winning five further Grand Slam doubles titles with Sweden's Jonas Bjorkman, and later he partnered the Indian player, Mahesh Bhupathi.

Mark Woodforde (right) lunges for the ball at the net while Todd Woodbridge moves to cover the ball if his partner misses.

Net or Not

At the start of a point, both teams have one player at the baseline: the server and the receiver. Once the point begins, they may choose one of several different formations. Two-up is where both players move to the net and is the favoured strategy of many professional doubles pairs. Two-up is a strong, attacking position, where points can be won by volleys but can sometimes be lost by the other team playing good lobs. Two-back is a highly defensive tactic, when a pair is forced back by the opposition. One-up, one back covers the depth of the court and may offer attacking chances, but it can also leave gaps for the opposition to exploit with angled shots.

STAT ATTACK

ITF Women's Doubles World Champions

2010 Gisela Dulko (Argentina) / Flavia Pennetta (Italy)

2009 Serena Williams (USA) / Venus Williams (USA)

2008 Cara Black (Zimbabwe) / Liezel Huber (USA)

2007 Cara Black (ZIM) / Liezel Huber (USA)

2006 Lisa Raymond (USA) / Samantha Stosur (Australia)

2005 Lisa Raymond (USA) / Samantha Stosur (Australia)

2004 Virginia Ruano-Pascual (Spain) / Paola Suarez (Argentina)

2003 Virginia Ruano-Pascual (Spain) / Paola Suarez (Argentina)

2002 Virginia Ruano-Pascual (Spain) / Paola Suarez (Argentina)

2001 Lisa Raymond (USA) / Rennae Stubbs (Australia)

Zi Yan volleys while Zheng Jie covers her shot. The pair became the first Chinese players to win a Grand Slam event in 2006 when they won the Australian Open.

Serving and Receiving

The net position is crucial in so many doubles points and servers aim to get their first serve in, even if they reduce its pace. This hopefully allows them to play serve and volley, coming in to the net to join their partners. Knowing this, the receivers are under pressure to hit a telling return. Most service returns aim to avoid the server's partner at the net by hitting the ball cross-court back at the server. The return is kept low to make it difficult for the opponent to volley. Occasionally, receivers may spot opponents moving across the net; this leaves a gap for them to hit the return down the line.

THE BIG COMPETITIONS

Whatever their age and level of ability, tennis players like to test themselves against others in tournaments. For the best professional tennis players around the world, this means getting on the major professional tours, rising up the rankings and taking part in the top tournaments.

On Tour

The men's and women's games each have their own organizations that run tours, a series of linked tournaments played around the world. The big tournaments offer masses of prize money and ranking points to those who do well, and are part of the professional tours run by the ATP for men and the WTA for women. Ranking points are awarded for how far a player progresses in a competition. Different tournaments have different amounts of ranking points at stake. The system is complex, but players can measure their progress against the world's elite by seeing how their position in the rankings has risen or fallen. Breaking into the upper levels of the rankings means that a player no longer needs to qualify for the biggest tournaments but, instead, has an automatic place.

End-of-Season Championships

Both the WTA and ATP tours have major end-of-season competitions limited to eight top players. Such is their high status, these championships are

Elena Dementieva in action with the Russian team that won the 2005 Fed Cup.

considered by some to be an unofficial fifth Grand Slam. In the women's game, this event is now known as the Sony Ericsson Championships and was won in 2006 by Justine Henin; Amélie Mauresmo was the 2005 champion. In the men's event, the Tennis Masters, Roger Federer, with three victories, and Australian, Lleyton Hewitt with two titles, are the most successful players in recent years.

Team Competitions

Tennis is essentially a game for individuals or pairs, but there are some important competitions for teams, too. The most famous is the Davis Cup, first held in 1900, for male players representing their country. Ties are held between two national teams of four players and consist of five matches, known as rubbers – two singles rubbers, then a doubles and, finally, two more singles contests. Winning teams can be promoted into the elite World Group of 16 nations that competes for the Davis Cup through knockout ties.

The Wightman Cup was the equivalent tournament for women until 1963, when it was succeeded by the Federation Cup (now called the Fed Cup). The Fed Cup follows a similar format to the Davis Cup, with five match ties but with the doubles rubber as the last match. The World Group is structured into a top eight and a second eight. In both competitions, the United States and Australia are the most successful nations, with 59 Davis Cup victories and 24 Fed Cup titles between them.

MAD FACT

Andy Murray and Rafael Nadal were the only players to beat world number 1 Roger Federer in 2006.

Andrew Murray became Britain's youngest ever Davis Cup player in 2005 at the age of 17. Ranked 533rd in the world in December, 2004, a year later he had risen to the world number 64. In 2007, Murray broke into the world's top ten for the first time.

THE AUSTRALIAN OPEN

The four biggest tournaments each year are known as Grand Slam events. These feature competitions for the world's leading men's and women's singles and doubles players, mixed doubles players and a range of junior and over 35s or veterans' competitions. The first Grand Slam on the calendar each season is the Australian Open, held every January.

Its History

First organized in 1905, the Australian Open was played on grass until 1988, when it moved to Melbourne Park (formerly known as Flinders Park). There, the tournament was played on the Rebound Ace court surface until 2008, when it was played on Plexicushion, a surface very similar to that used at the US Open (see page 40–41). The competition is played on a number of courts, the largest of which is named after the Australian Grand Slam legend, Rod Laver (see page 44). This court and the neighbouring Vodafone Arena have retractable roofs and are currently the only Grand Slam stadiums that do.

2006 mixed Doubles champions, Martina Hingis and Mahesh Bhupathi in action.

Hot, Hot Heat

Held in the height of the Australian summer, temperatures that can reach 40°C play a major part in the outcome of matches. The heat means that some players default (concede the match) as did Janko Tipsarevic when playing David Nalbandian in 2007. Introduced in 1998, the Australian Open has a special Extreme Heat Policy. This means that if the temperatures are severely high, no new matches will start on outside courts, and if matches are already underway, players are given a 10-minute break between each set.

Who is...

...Andre Agassi?

Half of American Andre Agassi's eight Grand Slams came at the Australian Open. Agassi began his career as the wild child of tennis and ended up as one of the sport's most-loved veterans. A baseline player who thrilled the public with his fast reactions and attacking instinct, Agassi slipped down the rankings in the mid-1990s and looked set for retirement. However, he stunned the tennis world with a great comeback, starting in 1998, which saw him win five Grand Slam titles, the last being the 2003 Australian Open.

Champions

Tennis balls bounce higher in hot weather, so players that like to hit high-bouncing shots tend to prosper in Australia. Baseline players such as Andre Agassi, Monica Seles and Steffi Graf have all done well, each winning the event four times. The 2007 tournament saw the return to form of Serena Williams, who was unseeded but triumphed, beating Maria Sharapova in the final. In the men's tournament, Fernando Gonzalez hit 91 aces throughout the tournament, but in the final could not defeat Roger Federer.

Andre Agassi poses with the men's singles trophy after winning the 2003 Australian Open.

THE FRENCH OPEN

Played in May and June, the French Open began as a tournament in 1891, but it did not open its courts to players from other countries until 1925. Three years later, the new Roland Garros stadium opened, named after a famous French fighter pilot who was killed in World War I. Following a major make-over of the stadium in 1999, the main court now has seating for just over 15,000 people.

MAD FACT

Only one Frenchman has won the men's singles title in the Open Era – Yannick Noah in 1983.

STAT ATTACK

Recent Men's Singles Champions

2011 Rafael Nadal

2010 Rafael Nadal

2009 Roger Federer

2008 Rafael Nadal

2007 Rafael Nadal

2006 Rafael Nadal

2005 Rafael Nadal

2004 Gaston Gaudio

2003 Juan Carlos Ferrero

2002 Albert Costa

2001 Gustavo Kuerten

Equal Pay

For many years, men's prize money has been greater than that awarded to women at most tournaments. However, in 2006 the French Open paid both the men's and women's singles champions the same amount. In 2007, all prize money was equal, from 14,290 euros for a player knocked out in the first round to a huge 1 million euros for the singles champions.

Clay Court Challenge

The slow clay courts of Roland Garros pose a special challenge to players who are more comfortable on faster surfaces. Clay encourages long rallies, often from the baseline, as both players move each other around the court seeking an advantage. Many players who have succeeded at the three other Grand Slams, Wimbledon and the Australian and US Opens, have found success at the French Open hard to come by. These include such tennis greats as Pete Sampras, Martina Hingis, Roger Federer and Lindsey Davenport, all of whom have won the other Grand Slams.

STAT ATTACK

Recent Women's Singles Champions

2011 Li Na

2010 Francesca Schiavone

2009 Svetlana Kuznetsova

2008 Ana Ivanovic

2007 Justine Henin

2006 Justine Henin

2005 Justine Henin

2004 Anastasia Myskina

2003 Justine Henin

2002 Serena Williams

2001 Jennifer Capriati

Who is...

...Justine Henin?

Standing just 1.67m tall, Justine Henin was one of the shortest players on the women's circuit but one of the best. Henin possessed a magnificent one-handed backhand that she used to send down scaring winners often from the back of the court. Although she had success on all types of court, the clay of the French Open has seen her win four Grand Slams there in five years. She has also won an Australian Open and one US Open title as well as a gold medal in the women's singles at the 2004 Olympics. Henin retired in 2008.

Record Breakers

The youngest winners of the French Open are 16-year old Monica Seles, who won in 1990, and Michael Chang, who at 17, won in 1989. Chris Evert has won the most French Open singles titles, with seven in total. Since Bjorn Borg's record six French Open titles between 1974 and 1981, no one man has dominated the French Open, although Ivan Lendl and Gustavo Kuerten have won the event three times each. In recent years, the men's singles has seen Argentinean, Brazilian and Spanish players do very well. The star among them is Rafael Nadal who has entered the French Open four times and won all four times.

Justine Henin moves forward to play a backhand shot during another successful defence of her French Open women's singles title.

WIMBLEDON

Established in 1877 by the All England Croquet and Lawn Tennis Club, Wimbledon is the oldest and most prestigious tennis tournament of all. Held in the last week of June and the first week of July, Wimbledon remains soaked in tradition. Competitors are referred to as Gentlemen and Ladies and are asked to wear mainly white clothing. The tournament is also now the only Grand Slam event to be played on grass.

Wimbledon's History

Wimbledon opened its tournament up to professional players in 1973 and today players compete in singles, doubles, mixed doubles and junior and veteran events. The top 32 men and women are seeded and 16 pairs are seeded in the doubles events. A number of the 128 places available in the singles draw are given to players directly (wild cards) or are competed for in the qualifying tournament held a week before Wimbledon starts.

On Court

Wimbledon is played on 19 courts: 16 'outside' courts and the three main show courts. Number Two Court is known as 'the graveyard of champions' as many seeded players, from Pete Sampras to Serena Williams, have been knocked out playing there. Number One Court is an 11,000-seater built in 1997, while Centre Court holds 14,000 spectators. Thousands more spectators congregate on the rising slopes of Aorangi Park to watch matches on a giant screen. The early English summer often means rain delays, which can see extra days played. By 2009, a renovated Centre Court will have a retractable roof to enable play to continue even through a downpour.

STAT ATTACK

Recent Wimbledon Singles Champions

	Men's	Women's
2011	Novak Djokovic	Petra Kvitova
2010	Rafael Nadal	Serena Williams
2009	Roger Federer	Serena Williams
2008	Rafael Nadal	Venus Williams
2007	Roger Federer	Venus Williams
2006	Roger Federer	Amélie Mauresmo
2005	Roger Federer	Venus Williams
2004	Roger Federer	Maria Sharapova
2003	Roger Federer	Serena Williams
2002	Lleyton Hewitt	Serena Williams
2001	Goran Ivanisevic	Venus Williams

Serena Williams chases down a ball during the 2004 tournament which was attended by 451,208 spectators.

STAT ATTACK

Wimbledon Records

Youngest champions

Men: Boris Becker (17 years old)

Women: Charlotte Dod and Martina Hingis (15 years old)

Youngest competitor

Jennifer Capriati (14 years old)

Oldest competitor:

Jean Borotra (65 years old)

Most Matches Played

Men: Jean Borotra (223)

Women: Martina Navratilova (326)

Fast Grass

Grass is the fastest of all the surfaces and can favour players with huge serves. Many of those who have prospered at Wimbledon are players who serve well and then come in to the net to volley. Grass also has an unpredictable, low bounce that makes it difficult to return serves. However, it can favour players who hit flat groundstrokes and sliced shots that skid on to their opponents.

Wimbledon Legends

Wimbledon has been the favourite setting for many tennis greats. Roger Federer, with five titles in a row, appears to be well on the way to joining the likes of Pete Sampras and Martina Navratilova. Sampras won seven singles titles at Wimbledon, while Navratilova has the most of all – nine. To those nine, she can add a further 11 doubles or mixed doubles titles. Navratilova shares the most titles record with Billie Jean King who, in 1973, completed a clean sweep at Wimbledon, winning singles, doubles and mixed doubles in the same year.

THE US OPEN

Held from late August into September, the US Open is the last Grand Slam of the season. It is hugely popular and noted for its brash atmosphere. In 2005, 659,538 spectators attended the US Open tournament.

Its History

The US Open, in many different forms, has been running for over 120 years. It opened to professional players in 1968 and moved to its present site at Flushing Meadows, New York City, in 1978. The main court in the 24,000-seat Arthur Ashe Stadium is named after the winner of the 1968 men's singles. In that year, there was a total prize money on offer of US$100,000. In 2006, over US$18.5 million was paid out to players, with a staggering US$1.2 million each to Roger Federer and Maria Sharapova, the winners of the men's and women's singles titles. Both men's and women's doubles winners pocketed US$400,000 per team, with the mixed doubles winners taking home US$150,000.

Maria Sharapova celebrates winning a crucial point.

STAT ATTACK

Recent US Open Singles Champions

	Men's	Women's
2011	Novak Djokovic	Samantha Stosur
2010	Rafael Nadal	Kim Clijsters
2009	Juan Martin del Potro	Serena Williams
2008	Roger Federer	Serena Williams
2007	Roger Federer	Justine Henin
2006	Roger Federer	Maria Sharapova
2005	Roger Federer	Kim Clijsters
2004	Roger Federer	Svetlana Kuznetsova
2003	Andy Roddick	Justine Henin
2002	Pete Sampras	Serena Williams

On Court

The US Open has been played on grass and, during the mid-1970s, on clay, but since 1978 it has been played on various hardcourt surfaces. The current surface is called Decoturf, a type of hardcourt with a concrete base and layers of rubber, acrylic and silica on top. The result is a fast (though not as fast as grass) surface with a lower bounce than other hardcourts. This means that some serve and volleyers have done well at the US Open, including Australian Pat Rafter, whose two Grand Slam successes were both US Opens. In 2005, the courts were given a colour makeover. The courts are now blue with a green outer court area, which supposedly makes it easier for players to see the ball. Unique amongst the Grand Slam events, the US Open insists on a tiebreaker system when the match goes into the fifth set.

Sampras hits an overhead smash at the US Open. His first Grand Slam success came at the US Open in 1990 when he beat Ivan Lendl, John McEnroe and Andre Agassi on the way to the title.

Who is...

...Pete Sampras?

Throughout the 1990s and early twenty-first century, there was often only one man to beat at the US Open and Wimbledon, and he was Pete Sampras. His serve was powerful, accurate, well-disguised and held up under pressure. His second serve was almost as good as his first. Sampras backed up his serving by being one of the best players at the net, as well as possessing magnificent forehand drives and overhead smashes. His serve and volley game saw him win five US Opens and a record seven Wimbledon titles.

MAD FACT

The great Bjorn Borg holds the unenviable record of having reached the final four times without winning, the same record as Evonne Goolagong Crawley in the women's singles.

Winners and Losers

American winners are especially well remembered at the US Open. Andre Agassi won the men's singles title twice and completed a remarkable 21 appearances in a row. Jimmy Connors appeared at 22 US Opens and won a record 98 matches and five singles titles. Chris Evert won six women's singles titles, while her great rival, Martina Navratilova, won an incredible 16 US Open titles – four singles, nine doubles and three mixed doubles.

GRAND SLAM LEGENDS

There have been many amazing and memorable players who have won a number of Grand Slam events throughout their careers. Here are five of the most notable winners.

Rod Laver

The 'Rockhampton Rocket' was the greatest player of the 1960s and, some say, of all time. Small and light, standing only 1.72m tall and weighing about 68kg, Australia's Laver relied on superb timing and footwork as well as a shrewd tactical brain to triumph over opponents. He remains the last male player to win all four Grand Slam singles titles in a single year, a feat he achieved twice, in 1962 as an amateur and in 1969 as a professional.

STAT ATTACK

Longest Winning Streak of Matches in Open Era

Men

46 – Guillermo Vilas

44 – Ivan Lendl

43 – Bjorn Borg

43 – Novak Djokovic

42 – John McEnroe

Women

74 – Martina Navratilova

66 – Steffi Graf

58 – Martina Navratilova

57 – Margaret Smith Court

55 – Chris Evert

Bjorn Borg

Known for his ice-cool temperament and stunning baseline technique, Bjorn Borg played in the Davis Cup for Sweden aged just 15 and won his first Grand Slam, the 1974 French Open, just two years later. He became a sensation, defending his title the next year and then winning four French Opens (1978–81) and an incredible five Wimbledon titles (1976–80) in a row. His epic matches with the more hot-headed Jimmy Connors and John McEnroe have passed into legend.

Steffi Graf

The German player emerged as the most serious challenger to Martina Navratilova in the mid-1980s, and in August 1987 Graf became ranked world number 1. The following year she achieved an unprecedented Golden Slam – winning all four Grand Slam tournaments in the same year and adding an Olympic gold medal to the wins. In total, she won a staggering 22 Grand Slam singles titles and one doubles title – the 1988 Wimbledon women's doubles with Gabriela Sabatini. Graf retired in 1999, and two years later married Andre Agassi.

Billie Jean King

Billie Jean King was an American who pioneered women's tennis and helped found the first fully professional tour for women in the 1970s. King won 12 Grand Slam singles titles, including six Wimbledon singles and four US Open titles. She won a further 27 Grand Slam titles, 16 in women's doubles and 11 in mixed doubles – an epic achievement. A tireless supporter of women's tennis, King later coached Fed Cup and Olympic teams. In 2006, the home of the US Open tournament was renamed the Billie Jean King National Tennis Center in her honour.

Boris Becker

The youngest ever male winner of Wimbledon, Boris Becker fought out many memorable matches with players such as Ivan Lendl, Pete Sampras and Stefan Edberg. His big serve, which earned him the nickname 'Boom Boom' and his all-action style gained him many fans and ignited the sport in his home country of Germany. During his career he won 15 doubles titles and 49 singles, including triumphing at Wimbledon three times, the Australian Open twice and the US Open once. Preferring fast courts, he found the French Open tougher, although he did reach the semi-finals on three occasions.

GLOSSARY

Ace   A serve that the opposing player is unable to return.

Approach shot   A shot used from inside the baseline to enable a player to come to the net.

ATP   Short for the Association of Tennis Professionals, it is the organisation that runs men's professional tennis.

Backspin   Hitting the underside of the ball so that, when it bounces, the ball brakes and bounces up.

Baseline   The back line of the court which marks out the court's length.

Cross-court   A shot hit diagonally across the court rather than one hit straight over and down the line.

Double fault   A point lost when the server fails to get either of his or her two serves in play.

Drop shot   A delicate shot that just clears the net and falls short in the opponent's court.

Grand Slam   A term used to describe the four biggest tournaments of the year – the Australian, French and US Opens plus Wimbledon. It also means to win all four of these tournaments in a single year.

Groundstroke   Any shot played after the ball has bounced.

Lob   A high shot played so that the ball travels over an opponent's head and into the court behind him or her.

Match point   A point which, if won, results in a player or doubles pair winning the entire match.

Open Era   The period since 1968 where all players, including paid-to-play professionals, were allowed to enter tournaments.

Rally   An exchange of shots between the players in a point.

Seed   The top players in a tournament (usually the first 16 or 32) who are prevented from playing one another in the earliest rounds of a competition.

Serve and volley   A style of play that involves rushing towards the net immediately after the serve, in order to make a volley off the return.

Service box   The rectangular area on the other side of the net in which a serve must land in order to be legal.

Service break When one player wins a game while the other player is serving.

Tie break The system used in many competitions to end a set after the scores are tied at six games each.

Topspin Hitting over the top of the ball to make it spin forward.

Tramlines The area on either side of the singles court that enlarges the court when doubles is played. It is also sometimes known as the alley.

Umpire The official in charge of a tennis match.

Unforced error A mistake which usually leads to a player losing the point rather than being brought about by his or her opponent's good play.

Unseeded The players in a tournament who are outside of the top 16 or 32, depending on the tournament.

Volley Playing the ball in the air before it bounces.

WTA Short for the Women's Tennis Association, it is the governing body of women's professional tennis.

WEBSITES

WWW.LTA.ORG.UK/

Homepage of the Lawn Tennis Association, the organization that runs tennis in the UK.

WWW.TENNISAUSTRALIA.COM.AU

Home on the internet of Tennis Australia, this website includes information on local clubs, players and coaches and tournaments, including the prestigious Australian Open.

WWW.WTATENNIS.COM

The official internet site for the Women's professional tennis tour, the WTA. Here you can read in-depth news, competitions and player profiles.

WWW.ATPTENNIS.COM

Homepage of the Men's professional tour, the ATP. This site includes biographies and a wealth of statistics on many of the world's highest-ranked male players.

WWW.WIMBLEDON.ORG

The official website of the Wimbledon championships with details of past tournaments and stories about the competition's classic matches.

WWW.ONTENNIS.COM/

A good general site for tennis, containing the basic rules of the game, player and competition news and information on diet, some shots and the game's history.

HTTP://SPORTS.ESPN.GO.COM/SPORTS/TENNIS /INDEX

An excellent tennis news site with lots of features on tournaments, players and schedules and results.

Note to parents and teachers:

Every effort has been made by the publishers to ensure that these websites are suitable for children, that they are of the highest educational value, and that they contain no inappropriate or offensive material. However, because of the nature of the Internet, it is impossible to guarantee that the contents of these sites will not be altered. We strongly advise that Internet access is supervised by a responsible adult.

# INDEX